LOVE ME TENDER

TOM HOLLOWAY

Inspired by Euripides'
Iphigenia in Aulis

Currency Press, Sydney

First published in 2010
by Currency Press Pty Ltd,
PO Box 2287, Strawberry Hills, NSW, 2012, Australia
enquiries@currency.com.au
www.currency.com.au
in association with
Company B Belvoir, Sydney.
Reprinted 2014, 2018

NATIONAL LIBRARY OF AUSTRALIA CIP DATA

Author: Holloway, Tom.
Title: Love me tender: inspired by Euripides' Iphigenia in Aulis /
               Tom Holloway.
ISBN: 9780868198699 (pbk.)
Series: Current theatre series.
Subjects: Australian drama – 21st century. 2009 – Drama.
Dewey Number: A822.4

Contents

Typeset by Dean Nottle for Currency Press.
Cover design by Tim Kliendienst.
Cover photograph by Michael Corridore.

Currency Press acknowledges the Traditional Owners of the Country on
which we live and work. We pay our respects to all Aboriginal and Torres
Strait Islander Elders, past and present.

Love Me Tender was first produced by ThinIce, Company B Belvoir and Griffin Theatre Company in association with Perth Institute of Contemporary Arts (PICA) at PICA Performance Space, on 24 February 2010, with the following cast:

Colin Moody, Belinda McClory, Luke Hewitt
Kris McQuade and Arky Michael

Director, Matthew Lutton
Set & Costume Designer, Adam Gardnir
Sound Designer, Kelly Ryall
Lighting Designer, Karen Norris

NOTE ON THE PLAY

This play is for any number of actors.

Place: ?

Time: ?

THANKS

I would like to thank Griffin Theatre Company, Company B, ThinIce, Nick Marchand, Matthew Lutton, Peter Matheson, Zilla Turner and HLA Management, Mel Kenyon and Casarotto and Ramsey Associates, the original cast and crew, and all my family and friends. But most importantly, I would like to thank my wife Elin Eriksen.

Tom Holloway

1: SORROW AND JOY

– Right. As he… I don't know… runs through the building, he sees the sun shining in low and… and… bright?

– Okay. Yes. As you run through the building you see the sun shining in low and bright. Okay?

– As I run through the building I see the… morning?

– Yes. Good.

– Morning sun shining in, low and bright. Right.

– As he hears the screams up ahead he sees the sun hit the dust in the air, like… yes?

– Pillars?

– Yes. Like pillars of… umm…

– Golden?

– Yes! Like pillars of fine floating flakes of golden snow. Yes. Good! And as he runs down the hall and hears the screams. The terrible screams. The pillars. The pillars of fine, floating flakes of golden snow, capturing the first rays of the morning sun, they are ripped apart into… into…

– Chaos?

– Ripped apart into chaos?

– Billowing?

– Yes!

– The pillars are ripped apart into billowing chaos.

– The screams… The cries…

– As you run down the hall you rip the pillars apart.

– Yes.

– The pillars of fine, floating, flakes of golden dust. You rip them apart into billowing chaos and the screams. The cries…

– Yes. I hear the screams and the cries. I see the low morning sun and the dust in the air and I run. Run hard? Yes. Run hard towards the screams and the cries coming from a room up ahead.

– The sun on his face.

– The sun warm on your face.

– The sun, bright in my eyes.

– His footsteps echo.

– Yes. No. No. His footsteps don't echo. His footsteps are drowned out by the deafening screams coming from the room up ahead!

– Yes! Good!

– Your footsteps. As you run down the hall your footsteps are drowned out by the loud, terrifying and passionate screams coming from the room up ahead.

– Right. I can't hear anything. I can't hear a single thing. I can't hear my footsteps as I run. I can't hear my… yes? My heart? Yes?

– Yes!

– I can't even hear my own heart pounding in my own chest with my own blood. My own blood rushing through my body. I can't hear my breath. My rasping breath making my chest heave. As I see the rising sun hit the dust like pillars of golden snow in front of me all I hear is the deafening and passionate screams from the room up ahead. Yes?

– Yes!

– Yes!

– Thank you.

– Heaves… that's good. Heaves is good!

– Yes.

– Thank you. And?

– And?

– He gets to the room.

– You get to the room.

– I… right…

– He can hear it.

– I hear it.

– You hear it.

– His wife.

– Your wife.

– Hooves? Do I hear hooves?

– Not yet.

– Right.

– As he gets to the room he hears the terrifying cries of his wife and the voice of a man in there with her.

– You stand at the door to the room and through it you hear the cries of… the terrifying and passionate cries of your wife and the voice of a man who is, yes, in there with her.

– I stand at the door to our bedroom. My bedroom. My wife's bedroom. And through the door I hear her in there crying out. Screaming. Crying out in… screaming as if… And a man. I hear a man with her too. Yelling. Shouting.

– He pants from running.

– Pants?

– Yes.

– No. You heave. Not pants. Okay?

– Yes.

– You heave from running. Your breath heaves.

– Of course!

– Fast. Deep. And you taste sweat on your lips.

– And I open the door.

– You push the door open.

– He bursts into the room.

– I push the door open and I burst into the room.

– He sees in front of him. His wife. On the bed. Naked. Sweat. Covered in sweat. And a man. A man between her legs.

– You see. Do you hear this? Yes. Yes this is… you see in front of you. Your wife. On the bed. Naked. Yes? Sweating. Writhing. Yes?

– Writhing. Good.

– Yes, writhing on the bed. And there is a man between her. There between her legs in front of you.

– I see this. I see her on the bed. I see her body. Her skin. I see him. A man. There in front of me between her legs and I am… my chest heaves and I taste sweat on my lips and I see this. I stand there and see this and…

– And his wife.

– And your wife.

– And my wife.

– She reaches out to him.

– She sees you and reaches out to you.

– Reaches out to me?

– Yes. For help. She reaches her hand out for you as a sign. A call. A desperate call for help.

– Right. She reaches out in desperate need of help.

– Yes.

– The pains of labour…

– Right.

– The terrifying and passionate pains of labour shoot through her eyes.

– Good.

– He moves to her.

– You move to her.

– I. Yes. Of course. I move to her.

– He rushes over to her.

– You don't hesitate. You move straight to her. Straight over to her.

– Yes. I rush. I rush over and I take her hand and hold it. Hold it tightly.

– And he sees…

– And you see…

– And I see the wildness of labour shooting through her eyes.

– Yes.

– Good!

– And he thinks…

– And you think…

– And I think. This is it. This is the moment.

– Her… his wife… Her face full of pain and… I don't know.

– Anticipation?

– Yes!

– Ecstasy?

– Yes! Full of pain and anticipation and ecstasy. Yes! And the screaming is louder. Is reaching… yes? Is reaching its peak. He can tell the screaming is reaching its absolute peak!

– You can tell. These two in front of you. Her hand. Her sweat. The pain. The pleasure. Him. Calling out. You can tell it is all reaching its absolute peak!

– Yes! I see all that! The screams ringing in my ears. The sweat on my lips. I think this is… just as it is all reaching… just as I can tell from the screams and the breathing and the cries that it is all reaching its absolute peak… Once more I notice here in this room… The sun. Suddenly once more I notice the early morning sun shining in hitting the dust, but there are no pillars in this room. No pillars of floating flakes of golden snow and stillness. No. There is none of that! There is just chaos! All around there is simply wild billowing chaos! Yes?

– Yes!

– Yes!

– And then?

– Yes. And then!

– Then the man cries out. It's happening!

– The man cries out that he can see it coming!

– I'm looking all around at the dust and the chaos. The wild chaos. And the man. He screams out. It's coming. He can see her coming!

– He stands there clenching his wife's hand with his heart pounding in his chest and his wife screaming and straining as the man calls out he can see the baby coming!

– You stand there and your chest is pounding and you're covered in sweat and your wife, she's writhing. Writhing there naked on the bed as the man calls out he can see your baby coming. He can see the head breaching!

– I see. There is hay everywhere and now it has started so as I stand here with my wife, she... yes. He calls out he can see the head coming!

– And then. Like that!

– Then suddenly!

– Yes?

– She comes out!

– Comes out?

– What?

– Just 'comes out'?

– She is born!

– Yes! You see her born!

– I see my little girl born!

– Yes. Much better. Not comes out. Is born! Suddenly she is born!

– You see her, yes? You see her head and then body and then legs and you see her born.

– There in front of you. You see the man holding your new little girl.

– I see the man with my new little darling. Helping her.

– The cord is cut.

– The screams subside.

– Her fur and hooves. Now I see her hooves. Wet with placenta and blood. So much…

– He. He sees his daughter for the first time and he is suddenly. In this moment. Suddenly filled with this great and sudden sense of… yes? Of… yes? Of overwhelming… yes? Of overwhelming…

– You see your daughter for the first time and you are suddenly filled with. In that moment you are suddenly filled with this overwhelming sense of… This crippling sense of… yes? Crippling. Of…

– I see her for the first time. Her fur. Her hooves. She is on the ground amongst the hay. Straw sticking to her wet, furry body as she struggles to stand and clumsily take her first steps. And as I see this I am filled with this feeling of… of… yes?

– He sees his wife and his daughter and as he sees this he suddenly realises he knows love… Yes. Love. He knows love like he has never known it before. He feels joy like he has never felt it before. Joy!

– No! Not love! You see your wife and your daughter there together and you are filled with an immense and crippling wave of pain and horror and sorrow like nothing you have ever felt before. Nothing. Because. Because you can see. You know what will. You can sense what you are one day going to

– I see her. There amongst the hay. Struggling to stand. My wife lying, still, and her. Our deer. She looks up at me with her black, blank eyes and I feel like she is suddenly looking straight at me. Deep into me. I see those big eyes of hers look straight into me and I feel it deeply. I feel it suddenly and deeply inside me and as she looks deep into me it is as if I get these flashes. These amazing and yet terrible flashes of what is to come and suddenly I am filled with an immense and overwhelming sense of love and horror. Yes. Of pain and happiness. Yes. Of joy and sorrow. Yes. Of immense joy and of absolute sorrow. Yes.

2: SAVIOUR / SACRIFICE

– Ah, yes. Lovely. Isn't that lovely?

– Ah, yes.

– A miracle. That's what that is.

– No doubt.

– You know?

– Absolutely.

– The miracle of life.

– Yes.

– It gets me every time.

– Me too.

– And it's a good time to bring a life into the world.

– Yes.

– I think it's a lovely time to bring a new life into the world.

– Isn't it?

– It is. I would say actually. The best time to bring a new life into the world.

– You think?

– Oh yes.

– Me too.

– You do?

– Oh yes.

– Good. Yes. I think it is the best time to bring a little girl into the world.

– Girl?

– Especially a girl.

– Oh yes?

– Oh yes.

– Oh yes.

– The opportunities.

– Exactly.

– The learning.

– I know.

– The sense of, yes? The only time in the history of the human race there has ever been such a sense of... of...

– Of... ummm...

– Equality! The only time in the history of the human race there has ever been such a sense of equality!

– Oh, yes.

– You know what I mean?

– Absolutely.

– It is a woman's world.

– Yes.

– More than at any other time.

– Yes. It certainly is a good time to bring a new girl into the world.

– She could lead a country. Run a bank. A church. A multinational corporation. An...

– An underground movement?

– Sorry?

– A movement?

– Yes. I guess. An underground movement fighting hard against...
even against a multinational corporation. That is how many
opportunities there are today, you know?

– Yes. Animal rights?

– Yes. Absolutely. She could be a rebellious animal rights fighter that
causes... that inflicts...

– Terrorist?

– Yes! Terrorist attacks against zoos freeing all the animals into the
streets of some big city.

– Or zoo keeper?

– Well, she loves animals. Little deer and things. So why not?

– Exactly.

– She could be anything, is the point.

– A martyr?

– Yes. A martyr for some great cause, sacrificing herself for... for...

– Some great cause?

– Yes. So many opportunities.

– A marathon?

– Sorry?

– Could she run a marathon?

– Without doubt. A half marathon. A full marathon that takes her
across some kind of... I don't know... famous bridge?

– Yes. The Sydney Harbour Bridge.

– Exactly. Or the Golden Gate.

– The Brooklyn?

– Absolutely. She can go anywhere. Anywhere in the world. The east. The south. The west. The north. Police stations. Churches. Board rooms. Parliament houses. Strip joints. She can happily walk into a strip joint as a customer without anyone batting an eyelid. Happily walk in and order a beer and sit back and enjoy the show without a single person batting an eyelid. Money. She can sit up the front and put money in the g-strings and no-one will ask why. Will ask how. No-one will even bat an eyelid. That is how good it is today for a woman to be born. There is real… what's the word? Hope! Yes! There is real hope for a girl entering this world now!

– Isn't there?

– You know what I mean?

– Oh, yes!

– Real and true hope!

– Yes!

– The world is their oyster!

– There's no doubt!

– It is theirs to conquer!

– Absolutely!

– To rise to the top of!

– Yes! Without a doubt!

– For thousands and thousands and tens of thousands of years there has been no better time for a girl to be born into the world.

– Absolutely.

– So we must protect them.

– Yes.

– Keep them safe.

– Yes.

– Teach them.

– Yes.

– Show them they can do anything.

– Oh yes.

– But keep them safe.

– Yes. Of course.

– Because, you know...

– Yes.

– There are many threats out there.

– Aren't there?

– There really are.

– I know.

– At every turn!

– Everywhere you look!

– I mean you can't turn. Can't turn your head without seeing a whole array of wild and dangerous threats. And to a girl? For a young girl? The threats are tenfold for a young girl these days.

– Aren't they just?

– My word they are.

– It's frightening.

– Yes. It's frightening how dangerous it can be for a young girl out there in this day and age.

– Absolutely.

– You know what I mean?

– Yes.

– I mean in the church, in the school, in the workplace, in the park, in the home. Who knows where a young girl is safe these days.

– There's nowhere.

– Not really. You're right. There's really nowhere a young girl can truly be safe these days.

– No.

– Safe to just grow up, you know?

– I know.

– And that's important.

– Yes.

– To be able to just grow up. At your own pace. In your own way. But for a girl? For a young girl? A little girl with big doe-y eyes and long eyelashes? Where's she meant to do it?

– I know. And such beautiful eyes.

– Yes. I mean, it's not... you know. Not like in the old days.

– It isn't, is it?

– Not at all.

– No.

– I mean in the old days life was simpler.

– Yes.

– More innocent.

– I know.

– Safer.

– Without a doubt.

– Especially for a young girl.

– Yes. Life in the old days was a lot safer for a young girl.

– You know what I mean?

– Yes.

– I mean, these days…

– Yes.

– Predators. There are predators everywhere.

– I know.

– Everywhere you look.

– Absolutely.

– And what do they want?

– The predators?

– Yes. What do the predators want?

– Young girls?

– Yes! Exactly! Young girls! Hiding everywhere just waiting to pounce on some innocent young girl.

– Everywhere.

– It's almost. I mean there are so many it is almost impossible to keep your children safe these days.

– Yes.

– You can almost guarantee danger will come into their lives.

– Yes.

– I mean it's the norm, really.

– Isn't it?

– It sure is.

– The things that can happen to them…

– It's scary.

– Yes.

– What might be done to them…

– Yes.

– To their little bodies…

– Their hooves. Their fur.

– To their minds and souls.

– Traps and guns and poachers and other animals. Getting their little
hoof caught in some long forgotten rusted, metal trap. Getting shot.
Shot for some illegal black market poacher that wants to skin her
and gut her and sell her at a local market. Other animals. Scary
animals that might attack her to feed their young. Kill something
young to keep something else young alive. You know what I mean?
And with that… With all that… You never know what will happen
to them.

– And they are so helpless.

– Yes.

– So defenceless.

– I know.

– Which is why they are preyed upon so much.

– Yes.

– You know?

– Absolutely.

– It is like. I mean it is so common it is like we have sold them out or
    something.

– Burnt them at the stake.

– For our own sins.

– Yes.

– You know?

– But they taste so good.

– Sorry?

– They taste so sweet.

– They do, don't they?

– Absolutely.

– Juicy.

– Yes. So tender and juicy.

– Succulent.

– Yes.

– They are succulent like nothing else. Like no other...

– Mmmm.

– Delicious.

– Yes. I mean once they get older they can really dry out, you know?
    Become tough and dry. But those young ones... those juicy young
    ones...

– My mouth's watering just thinking about it.

– Yes! I mean I know sometimes the practices. The methods used
    to get them like that are questionable. Sometimes there are very
    questionable methods used that some people would even call cruel,
    you know?

– Yes.

– Like torture I guess. I guess some people would even call it torture.

– Indeed.

– But it's so succulent and delicious that to be honest I just don't care!

– Oh, it's so tasty!

– I want some right now!

– Me too!

– Shall we go and get some?

– Now?

– Yes.

– I do want to!

– Me too!

– Yummy!

– I know a place. A wonderful place.

– Really?

– Yes. They get them fresh. Straight from the parks and homes and churches and schools and straight onto the plate for us!

– Really?

– Yes!

– That does sound delicious. From the homes too?

– Oh, yes!

– I do love the ones that come from the homes.

– Yes, they are especially delicious.

– Yes!

– Let's go!

– Yes let's!

– So delicious!

3: A MOMENT OF TENDERNESS / LULLABY TO HIS BABY

– Each day I'll do a golden deed
By helping those who are in need
My life on earth is but a span
And so I'll do the best I can

Life's evening sun is sinking low
A few more days and I must go
To meet the deeds that I have done
Where there will be no setting sun

To be a child of you each day
My life must shine along the way
I'll sing your praise while the ages roll
And strive to help some troubled soul *

CHORUS: 'Next I Saw the Countless Fleet'

I'm a cop, right? It's my job. It's just my job. But it means I see things. I sit there in the patrol car and I drive around the streets of this town both day and night, yeah? And I go everywhere... The good parts of town, the bad parts of town... And so I see... Well... everything. Really. Everything. You know what I mean? All kinds. All sorts. And the thing is, you see... I see us. You and me. I see us doing amazing things. Saving. Rescuing. Loving. Caring. Supporting. Sacrificing. Going without. Working hard. Being there for each other. Being pretty bloody amazing to each other. Really. Amazing. But I also see... because of my job... I also see us... I see us like... as if we were animals. As if we're still animals. Tearing. Ripping. Killing. But worse. Worse than animals because they have a need. Some kind of need. You know? But us? But for us? And that makes me ask myself this question... If we do all that... If that is what we're really like... Good and bad and all that... How do we cope with that? How do we try to come to terms with something like that?

---

* Slightly adapted from the American gospel song 'A Beautiful Life'. Lyrics by William M. Golden (1918).

4: THE FATHER DEFENDS HIMSELF

– So. The other day. I was playing with her. You know? Playing in her
bedroom with her.

                                                         – Playing with her?

– Yes.

                                                         – In her bedroom?

– Yes.

                                                         – Right.

– Why?

                                                         – Nothing.

– Sure?

                                                         – Of course.

– Okay. So we're playing in her bedroom and we're rolling around.
Laughing. Tickling. That kind of thing. On her bed.

                                                         – Right.

– You know?

                                                         – Yes.

– Rolling around on her bed.

                                                         – Right.

– So…

                                                         – Yes.

– And she's on top of me.

                                                         – Right.

– I'm on my back and she's on top of me. Sitting on me. Her body.
Her little body. And I have my hands on her. Holding her. And she's
got her hands on my chest. Leaning on my chest. You know?

                                            – Right. Okay. Sounds…

– What?

                                                        – Nothing.

– Sounds what?

                                                        – Like fun.

– Right. Well. It was.

                                                        – That's all.

– Yes. Well. You know?

                                                            – Yes.

– We've been rolling around and tickling and laughing and all that
kind of thing and there she is sitting on me. Above me. Her hands
on me. My hands on her. And she looks at me. Looks at me like…
gives me this look like…

                                                    – Like what?

– Like… I don't know… I can't really…

                                                            – Say?

– No. I can't really say.

                                                        – Right.

– But I got filled with this… this feeling, like… like… I don't know.
This immense

                                                    – Immense?

– Yes.

– Jesus.

– I know. Immense.

– Right.

– And she looked at me like that. Looked down on me. And she put her hand. Moved her hand up and put it on my face and the feel of her skin. Her soft skin against my cheek… So warm and soft, you know?

– Right.

– I mean, it felt…

– Good?

– So good.

– Yes.

– Her skin is so… is completely…

– Sure.

– So I'm feeling that, right?

– Yes.

– And it feels really…

– Yes.

– So I close my eyes.

– Really?

– Yes. I just lay there and closed my eyes and felt her hand on my cheek and it was like… it was just…

– Wow.

– It was so much more than…

– Right.

– And I opened my eyes and looked into her… looked straight into her big… beautiful big… and then I saw it.

Saw it?

– Saw what it was all about.

– Right.

– What made me see this is more than the usual…

– Right.

– I saw that we need each other.

– What?

– It felt like we really. As we looked into each other's eyes. Like we really need each other. Her, me and me

– Right.

– Her.

– Right.

– That's what it was like.

– Really?

– Yes. And we do. We do need each other.

– Of course. I guess.

– You know?

– Yes.

– And she leant down and put her arms around me and… I mean this. Kissed me. Kissed me on the lips. Soft. Gentle. You know? She lay on top of me and looked at me like that and then leant down and kissed me on the lips and I. Well. I kissed her back. I kissed her too, because… because… And I. I put my arms around her and held her and kissed. Her head was right there so I breathed her in and kissed her and told her I loved her and she said. She told me she loved me too and we lay there like that and it was... it was so...

– Right.

– You know?

– Yes.

– And we do love each other. We really...

– Of course.

– You know?

– Sure.

– You know?

– She's your girl, so...

– Yes.

– Your little girl. Yes?

– Exactly.

– So of course you do.

– But more than that. I think we have something special.

– You and her?

– Yes.

– Right.

– Do you know what I mean?

– Sure. I think. Sure.

– And I want that. I want to be able to have that forever. I don't want anything to get in the way of her and me and what we have because it is the strongest. I mean the absolute strongest thing I have ever felt.

– Right.

– And I want that forever.

– Of course.

– You know?

– Who wouldn't?

– Yes.

– How old is she now?

– Three.

– Right.

– I think we understand each other.

– Right.

– In a deep and spiritual way.

– Spiritual?

– It's the only word that can

– Right.

– Get close.

– Sure.

– You know?

– Right. Spiritual. Right.

– Yes.

– Right.

– And you know what? What's so wrong with

– Sorry?

– You know what's so wrong with the world?

                                          – The world?

– Yes.

                                               – What?

– What did you think about me being on my daughter's bed with her?

                                            – What?

– About all that? What were you thinking about all that?

                                          – All that?

– What I just told you.

                                    – What do you…

– What do I mean?

                                           – Yes.

– You know what I mean.

                                    – No, I…

– You didn't think… just for a moment… you didn't question why I was on the bed with my daughter?

                                            – Oh.

– Not for a moment?

                                    – No. Not at

– Yes you did.

                                    – No, I… I

– Yes you fucking… And that is… That. That is what's so… I mean a father can't even talk about… can't even say… without that coming up?

                                                                 – Right.

– I mean that's what people are like. That's what they think. The moment a father starts talking about his daughter, people straight away think

                                         – But, I didn't. I

– Come off it.

                                                       – I

– I mean I want to talk about how I love her. You know? I just want to be able to talk about how I

                                   – And you should be able

– Yes! I should be able to. I mean I'm her father. I'm her… so I should completely be able to stand here and talk about how much I love her. How I feel about her.

                                       – Yes. You should.

– But I can't, can I? I can't even

                                                 – Right.

– This world is…

                                                          – Yes.

– You know?

                                                          – Yes.

– Because people… They're always thinking… the moment I was to start talking like that everyone's minds would always automatically go straight to… you know?

                                                            – Yes.

– Big-titted teen fucks twin sister.

                                                          – Yes.

– Milf fucks boy next door.

                                – Exactly.

– Dad teaches daughter how to

                                – Fuck and suck.

– What?

                                – Dad teaches daughter

– Right, so…

                                – Yeah.

– So when we sit here. When I try to talk about

                                – Love.

– Yes. The love I have for my daughter. Everyone's first thought goes
to dad teaches daughter how to fuck and suck because that… all
that… that is what they know.

                                – Yes.

– And that is

                                – Fucked.

– Yes. That is fucked.

                                – Yes.

– I mean…

                                – Yes.

– You know?

                                – Yes.

– It's totally…

                                – Yes.

– And it's where your thoughts went too.

                                                                    –

– Isn't it?

                                                                    –

– I know it is.

                                                        – Right.

– Because it's what you know too, isn't it?

                                                                    –

– That is what is fucked with the world.

                                                                    –

–

5: SHE TRIES TO TALK TO HIM / SHE IS ALONE

– Out on the perilous deep
  Where dangers silently creep
  And storms so violently sweep
  You're drifting too far from the shore

  Drifting too far from the shore
  Drifting too far from the shore
  Come to me today, let me show you the way
  Drifting too far from the shore

  Today the tempest rolls high
  And clouds overshadow the sky
  Sure death is hovering nigh
  Drifting too far from the shore

  Drifting too far from the shore
  Drifting too far from the shore
  Come to me today, let me show you the way
  Drifting too far from the shore *

---

* Slightly adapted from the American country gospel song 'Drifting Too Far from
  the Shore'. Music and lyrics by Charles E. Moody (1923).

6: THE STORY

– So, she loves the story?

– Stories. She loves stories.

– Oh, yes. So she loves stories?

– Of course. Well, at least she loves being told stories.

– Ah, I see. It's really just that she loves being told stories, not that she loves the actual stories?

– No. It's not that she loves the actual stories. It's not that at all. It's just she likes sitting there while someone tells her a story.

– Likes the attention?

– Yes. It's more like she just loves the attention.

– Well, who doesn't at that age?

– Exactly.

– You know?

– Yes. It's definitely not the story. I mean half the time there might as well not be any real story at all, you know?

– Right!

– I mean half the time you might as well just be there, talking… basically talking nonsense with her. Talking rubbish. You know? There's no need to follow strictly to traditional ideas of story because she's really not interested in it, you know? Narrative structure and all that.

– Right.

– I mean throw in a few characters here and there…

– Right.

– Like…

– Princesses…

– Exactly. Princesses. Princes. Kings. Queens. War.

– War?

– Well, you know. Some distant war about to break that only she can
help save by putting herself at… You know… really sacrificing
herself in some act of… of great heroism. That kind of thing.

– Right.

– And she's a girl, so…

– Right.

– So you know. Princesses. Princes. Kings. Queens. War. Love. Love
of course.

– Of course.

– The love of a prince. Of a kingly father. Of a queenly mother. A war
about love. Love sacrificed. Love that leads to great and terrifying
sacrifice.

– Yes.

– If you've got some of that in there, then you're fine!

– And animals, I imagine?

– What?

– Animals?

– Oh, yes. Right. Good point. Talking animals that help save her life
and that kind of thing.

– Right.

– But if you've got all that then really that's all you need.

– Right.

– I mean story like you and I know it, really isn't that important to her.

– Well, fair enough too I guess.

– Yes.

– I mean it's pretty limiting.

– You think?

– It can be.

– I guess.

– Yes.

– But as long as the ingredients are there, she loves it.

– Well, it's different these days, isn't it?

– What is?

– For them. At that age. Growing up. The amount of information they get exposed to and all that.

– Yes.

– It's different than it was for us.

– Good point.

– So story. Traditional ideas of story probably seem a little old or something.

– Maybe.

– You know? Like just a reference to something. Just some hint of story is enough of a reference because generally stories are so in us, it's like we know the famous ones well before we are ever directly exposed to them, you know?

– Right.

– It's kind of like they're deep inside us already, you know?

– Perhaps.

– So maybe that's why she's like that.

– Maybe. I mean, sure.

– You know?

– Yes. Or maybe she just likes the attention.

– Yes. I guess. Maybe it's just that.

– Maybe she just likes the voices he puts on and how often he makes himself look silly. Makes a fool of himself.

– Oh yes. I bet she loves that.

– She sure does.

– I bet she breaks out into laughter over that.

– Yes. She does love to laugh.

– And he sure can make her laugh.

– Yes.

– Everyone says it. Sees them in the street and things. They say how special the two of them seem together. How close.

– Right.

– How much he can make her smile.

– Right.

– You know?

– Yes. I guess.

– It's very lovely.

– Yes.

– Yes. Jealous. Everyone gets very jealous.

– It's just…

– Of the love. The love the two of them clearly have. People get very jealous of the love those two clearly share together.

– It's just he has these dark thoughts.

– Oh yes?

– Yes. It's just that he has these very dark thoughts.

– Like?

– He can't say.

– He can't?

– Right. Oh. Dark thoughts?

– Yes.

– Oh.

CHORUS: *'The Fiend of Strife'*

I scream to a halt at the field. My sirens are blaring. I see him. There in the field as the midday sun burns down from above. He is surrounded by cattle. He has a gun in his hand. Dead cows litter the ground. He points the gun again and shoots and another cow topples over. He has their blood on him. On his face and clothes and mixing with his sweat from the blistering hot sun. As I rush out of the car I see his eyes. Grey. Shallow. He doesn't squint from the brightness of the sun. He doesn't seem to feel the burn of it on his skin or the immense heat of it on his brow. He walks over and shoots another cow in the head. More blood. Again the animal falls to the ground. Again he does not flinch at the sound of the gun or the blood of the animal or by being faced with death that has come from his hands. This is not right. This is not what we are here for. This is not what drives us to get out of bed every day. As I see this in him I step out in the open, ignoring the heat and the burn and I stand there, exposed because I know this man isn't going to shoot me. I know he isn't going to shoot himself because this man is like any other. He is simply lost. He has simply forgotten what is right and wrong and who hasn't done that? Who has never felt that? He sees me through the heat like he is seeing me for the first time. Like he hasn't been aware of me or the lights or the siren until now. He lowers the gun. He walks over to me. He doesn't look me in the eyes. He hands me the gun and walks to the car and gets in the back and shuts the door. I tell dispatch I'm bringing him in. We drive in silence. I don't need to put handcuffs on him. I don't need to restrain him. When we get to the station he walks into the building and into the cell and lies down on the small bed. This is what he wants. This is what he needs. Our natures might vary, but he is the same as us. He just wants to be safe. He just wants to be looked after. He just wants right and wrong to be made clear to him.

7: WELCOME TO THE WIDE WORLD

– I watch them…
He asked me to stay.
He asked to do it alone.
Walk her to school alone.
Her first day.
Six years old and her first day into the wide world.
I stand in the window and watch them leave the house.
So proud.
Him so proud.
Glowing.
He looks down at her and he is glowing with pride.
Glowing with love.
They hold hands.
He reaches down and holds her hand.
She's sad.
She's been crying.
Scared.
Scared of what's out there.
Scared of leaving the home.
But he tells her…
He leans down and tells her…
The world is a wonderful place.
He tells her that.
The world is an amazing place and it will give you amazing things.
And he means it.
As he wipes away her nervous tears and says that to her he really
means it.
He wants her to go out into the world.
He wants everything to be wonderful for her.
And he wants it to be him that shows her.
He wants this walk to be just him and her.
He wants to be the only one holding her hand.
He wants to be the only one wiping away her tears.
He wants to be the only one guiding her out into the world.

He says it is his job.
He says he has to do it.
He says I have done enough and now it is his turn.
Now it is his turn.
Now I stand here at the window.
Now I look out at them.
Now I look out at everything and what I see is...
The things that I see are...

8: PARTY TIME!

– Hi there everybody!

– We're the Kids R Kool Dance Team!

– Who's ready to have a good time?!

– Yeah!

– Hands up in the air if you're a princess!

– Wooo!

– Hands up in the air if you're ready to do the Princess Dance!

– Oh yeah!

– Have you got your hair ready?

– Have you got your clothes ready?

– Who's got their sexy make-up on already?!

– Because we're going to do the Princess Dance!

– Every little girl wants to be a princess!

– Who wants to be a pop star?!

– Yeah!

– Pop stars are sexy!

– What, you're not dressed? Well we better put our party clothes on then!

– Everyone, start with the g-string!

– Now, slip into those hot fishnet stockings!

– Wriggle into that incy wincy little mini-skirt!

– Pull on those sexy knee-high, high-heeled boots!

– Don't forget your cut-off top!

– Got to show off that cute little midriff!

– Are your g-strings showing?!

– Now the lipstick!

– Now the blush!

– Now the nails!

– Now the eyelashes!

– Now you're beautiful!

– Now you're wonderful!

– Now you're the princess every girl really wants to be!

– Now we're ready to dance!

– Let's party!

– Yeah!

– Let's dance!

They do a dance to music. It is a blend of children's television and pole dancing. At times while dancing they yell out, 'Dance like a princess!'

9: WAR

– We see her. In the forest. She's on her own. Wandering. Wandering? Yes. Wandering alone through the forest. She sees the sun shine down from above like pillars? Yes, like pillars through the trees. It is quiet. Deeply quiet. It is the deep quiet of nature in the timeless moment of the mid afternoon. Yes. She is in the forest wandering and surrounding her are pillars of golden sunlight and the deep quiet of nature in the timeless moment of mid afternoon. We see her through the trees. Rummaging. Skipping and rummaging on the forest floor. Her big doe-y eyes. Her long lacey eyelashes. Yes? Yes? Yes. The ash stains her fur. The ash and charcoal stain her fur as she struggles. No. Staggers against the burnt dead trees. She is rummaging on the forest floor desperate to find anything to eat. Desperate to be free of the ash. Of the charcoal. The alien calls of firemen in the distance. Her legs collapse. As we see her wandering through the dead forest we see her legs collapse under her and the ash billow. Billow? Yes. Billow around her like floating flakes of snow. The trees are black. The earth is black and the light of the sun is dull with the ash that billows like fine flakes of snow. She is scared. We see her big, black eyes and she is alone in the dead forest and she is scared. The memory of the fire still filling her nightmares. The strange and alien sound of firemen and search-and-rescue teams echoing through the remains of her home. There is no-one to keep her safe. No-one to feed her. To protect her. No-one to guide her until she can reach an age where she can look after herself. We see her collapse into the ash and not get up. She can't move. She lies there. Starving. Scared. Desperate. Unable even to stand up because this world. This world that should be her world. That should give her what she needs. That should provide. Now suddenly offers her nothing. Gives her nothing.

10: THE MOTHER

– Hello.
I don't mean to
I don't normally come in to places like this.
Bars.
Pubs.
You know?
But I
Well I need to
To talk to a stranger
You know?
You know how sometimes you wish you could just
Just find someone
Someone you don't
That doesn't know you or
Or your situation
So you can just get some
Some stuff off your chest?
You know?
Well I just thought
Seeing you were sitting here
That it looked like you'd come here alone
So
Is that okay?

Right.
I can buy you
Get you a drink if you like?
Would that

Right.
It's my family you see
My husband.
I'm scared.
I shouldn't
I shouldn't really say that

But
You know
I think I'm scared.
It's not like
It's not that he's done anything
But he
The way he looks
The things that
That he says
You know?
He has to
He's got to go away and we don't
He doesn't know how long for and since he
I mean
Well
Ever since he found out
Something's happened.
Something's changed.
He's a good man.
Don't get me
He's a
He's one of those people other people look up to
You know?
I mean really look up to?
He's got an important place in the
In the community
You know?
He's a fire fighter and he has to go.
There are these huge
And he has to go to help but
And people admire him
Look up to
But they don't see.
They don't know the things I
They just don't.
He's a good husband
I mean distant
A little

And jealous too
He's always been a bit jealous.
Possessive.
And I liked that.
I used to really like that.
Like it meant
It showed
How much he loves me
You know?
But
We've got kids
You know?
Three kids.
But there's one
Our youngest
One that he
That he really
I mean
Dotes on.
He really dotes on her and they
The two of them
They have this very deep
Very special
Well
They're very close.
You know?
Sometimes
Sometimes I've even been jealous
Jealous of them.
Of what they have.
It's so
So lovely.
So loving.
So doting.
But
But what does that all
I mean now he has to go away
What does that all mean?

Why has he become so
I don't know
Why has he disappeared so much?
You know?
And he goes to
At times he goes to tell me
Like there's something he's thinking that he wants to
I really mean this
Like he wants to confess some kind of thoughts to me.
But something stops him.
Each time
Something stops him.
And I can't help
You know?
I can't help feeling something
Something bad
I can't help feeling something bad is going to come of all this.
I can't help but have this terrible feeling that something bad is
going to come of all this.
Something

I'm sorry to
That I disturbed you.
I'll leave.
I'll give the barman some money so you can
So you can get yourself some more drinks.
No
I insist.
Thank you.
I'll be
I'll get out of your hair now.
Thank you.

CHORUS: 'Dragging Men's Heads Backward to Cut Their Throats'

She screams drunkenly at me to get out of her house. She runs
at me and beats me against the chest. She falls to the floor. She
collapses at my feet. Screaming. Crying. Drunk. I step past her. I

need to make sure it is safe here. That no one is in harms way. It's
my duty when I am called out to disturbances like this. I step over
her and walk down the hall and in to the living room. She continues
to scream and cry behind me. I walk through the living room and
look in to each bedroom. I go to the kitchen and I look outside the
back window in to the garden. The light hits the dust in the air all
around me and this house. This home. Feels as if it is empty. As if
there was once a family that filled it. Pictures on the wall. Photos
of a man and a young girl. Things in the bedrooms. Toys. Clothes.
But now there is nothing. Nothing but a woman. A wife and mother.
Left alone. Now it seems like she is all that's left from what was
once in here. How did this happen? Why is she alone? I need to
know, how have we let that happen?

11: THE STORM THAT VIOLENTLY SWEEPS

– The sun is… The afternoon sun is shining?

– Yes.

– Right. So the afternoon sun is shining and there is no wind.

– No wind?

– No wind and so no breeze and so no relief, you see? And there hasn't been all day. No relief from the sun. As the afternoon grows long the heat does not diminish. The burn of the sun does not diminish so they just sweat there in the baking… baking late-afternoon sun?

– Which is why they went to the pool…

– Yes! Which is why they went to the pool in the first place!

– They are at the pool desperately hoping to get some relief after a day of the harsh baking of the sun.

– On a… this is right… on a day that is longer and more still than any day they have perhaps ever seen before.

– Right! Yes! Longer and more still than any day they have perhaps ever seen before!

– There are hundreds of people.

– There is a sea of people in the pool, yes.

– Yes. You can barely. You know? You can barely tell there is a pool there because it is so packed with people waiting, hoping for a break from the relentless still heat of the never-ending day.

– Yes. Like… Desperately waiting for someone to appease the angry gods.

– Gods?

– Yes. The angry gods that are refusing to release a breeze. Angry gods that seem almost to be punishing them all with the heat and the stillness...

– Yes. That's good. A sea of people in swimming costumes waiting desperately for someone to appease the angry gods...

– Thank you. They can feel it in fact. In the air. Through the thick, hot air. They had gone there expecting relief and happiness and joy and laughter and fun but what they have got. What they have encountered is a sea of people in desperate need for relief from the still heat that is... that is...

– Killing their sails!

– Yes. That is killing their sails! That is leaving their sails redundant.

– Yes.

– This is what they discover, the mother and daughter, as they arrive at the local pool after being called there by the father. They find the relentless stillness of the heat of angry gods.

– Yes. The air is thick with it.

– Yes. Stagnant.

– Yes. I like that. The air is stagnant with the anger of the gods.

– Yes the air is stagnant with an anger that could surely... That could surely... burn the forests down?

– Yes. That could surely cause the forests to burn. To char. To be instantly... So hot the forests, in fact, have already been instantly turned to ash. Yes?

– Nice. The air is so hot it has caused all the forests to instantly turn to ash. It has caused entire landscapes to be turned into flames and coal and ash.

– Like snow?

– Yes! Like hot snow floating through the remains of the forest. Very nice!

– Thank you.

– And the daughter has brought her toy.

– Yes. The daughter has brought her toy princess doll.

– Yes. No. Wait... No the daughter has not brought her doll. The daughter is not of an age to bring her doll. In fact the mother is surprised the daughter agreed to come to the pool at all because she... the daughter... is fast reaching the age where the last thing she wants to do is be seen with her parents at a pool.

– Yes. Exactly. The daughter is fast reaching the age in which she does not want to be seen with her parents at any kind of pool.

– Yes. So she hasn't brought a doll. She has, in fact, brought a friend. A male friend from the neighbourhood.

– What?

– I know...

– Boyfriend?!

– Well at least a boy that is a friend.

– Yes, I see! Good! This is very good! And they stand there in their costumes next to each other...

– The heat...

– The stillness...

– The anger...

– Yes, the anger...

– All the people...

– Hundreds of people.

– Yes. Hundreds of people all waiting there for… for something…
some kind of…

– And the girl. What? Ten? Is she ten? Eleven? Twelve?

– Yes.

– The girl that is ten-eleven-twelve. Just ten or eleven or twelve years
old stands there with the boy in the unrelenting afternoon heat and
feels… feels… what?

– Oh…

– A…

– A dread?

– Yes!

– As they stand there she feels a deep and terrible dread like nothing
she has ever felt before.

– Yes! Good!

– Isn't it?!

– Absolutely!

– And her father. Her father that called her mother and urged them to
come. Is standing there in front of them knowing full well that there
was nothing at the pool for them. Nothing but the anger of the gods.

– Yes. He stands there all the time knowing there was nothing at the
pool for them and as he stands there looking down on her. Not
being at the fires…

– Aha…

– Yes. Not being off where his community needs him…

– Exactly!

– Fighting the fires that are engulfing their city.

– Engulfing. Great!

– Thank you. As he stands there she sees a sense of… of… of… doubt!

– Yes!

– Yes! Of doubt in his eyes!

– That's great!

– She sees a sense of doubt in his eyes and she is suddenly overwhelmed with a deep and fearful sense of dread!

– Yes!

– Good!

– This is excellent!

– Yes!

– And his doubt is…

– His doubt comes from…

– Yes. His doubt comes from…

– As he stands there looking down on his daughter who is fast approaching the age of puberty, which seems… everyone says…

– Scientists.

– Doctors.

– Academics.

– Is getting younger and younger. Yes. How scientists and doctors and academics are all saying the age of puberty is getting younger and younger. The age of sexuality.

– Yes! How the age of sexuality is getting younger and younger and they… the experts… argue. Fiercely argue the cause of this.

– Fiercely. Nice.

– Thank you.

– Fiercely. Yes. Is it genetics? Is it something to do with genetics? Natural genetic modification or is it cultural? Is it due... yes? To cultural interference? To sex and sexuality filtering into the daily lives of young children and therefore, yes? Therefore. Those signifiers... Those...

– Dancers in mini-skirts.

– Yes!

– Pop songs about sex on the radio.

– Yes!

– Ads. Ads on television and the internet.

– Yes! Ads on the television and internet using sex to sell things at a younger... at an ever-younger age...

– Yes. Used to sell chocolate bars. Like eating a chocolate bar on an ad is really a lesson in fellatio, you know?

– Brilliant! That's what they say. That it's meant to remind us of fellatio.

– Yes.

– Sucking dick.

– Yes.

– Sucking hard cock.

– Hard cock. Yes!

– So ads using hard cock to sell chocolate bars or other ads selling... I don't know... make-up?

– Make-up kits for five-year-olds...

– Yes! Brilliant! Toy make-up kits for five-years-olds so they can put on lipstick and blush and all those things that are signifiers of sexual attraction!

– Flushed lips!

– Flushed cheeks!

– Wet pussies!

– Hard cocks!

– Yes! Ads about all those things that are advertised to children but are really about hard cocks and wet pussies when they are at an age where historically they would have no idea about... about...

– Fucking.

– Yes!

– So and So's famous sex tape.

– You're good at this!

– Porn.

– Right!

– Teen daughter taught to fuck and suck by father or

– Nice!

– Amateur video of teens fucking for first time.

– Exactly!

– High school girl punished for being naughty in all-team gang-bang.

– Brilliant!

– A ten-eleven-twelve-year-old girl walking into her father's office and finding him looking at a website called Young Tits Tight Asses.

– Tight asses. Yes!

– Dance troupes. Children's dance troupes who wear knee-high fuck-me boots and mini-skirts and whose make-up little girls can copy, learning how to look like a slut.

– Like a total slut.

– Age five and up.

– A total fucking slut!

– Yes.

– And the father. The father at his desk with his pants undone and his ten-eleven-twelve-year-old daughter running in to say hello. To give him a great big hug and a kiss and show him the mini-skirt she just got and the make-up job her best friend put on her and she's laughing and giggling and discovers her father there at the computer with his hand on his cock looking at photos of girls only just older than her. Only, what? A few years older than her and she sees him suddenly... stumble?

– Panic?

– What should he do first? Cover up the page or put his cock back in his pants?

– Which one is worse?

– Which one could be more damaging?

– So does nothing. Is so panicked he does nothing but sits there with his hand on his cock and the movie still playing of the girl being taught to fuck and suck by her daddy. There on the screen!

– Yes! He has doubt in his eyes!

– Yes! As he stands there in front of her at the pool with a boy that is a friend but means all those things, just a friend but still represents all those kind of things... He has a flash of doubt in his eyes!

– Yes!

– He has not yet left to fight the fires because he wanted this one moment with his family but now he is there, the smell of smoke in the air...

– As he stands there and sees her in a little bikini.

– Brilliant! A little bikini! Some tight little bikini!

– Tight, good! That's good. And I mean she is not yet... she has not yet hit puberty... but it is close. Months, perhaps? Months? A few years?

– Yes!

– Yes. So. Is perhaps just months away and he sees her there and in that moment he has a flash of doubt and...

– Yes?

– Because...

– Yes?

– What is the boy thinking?

– The boy, yes!

– Has he reached puberty already? Is he already thinking about being more than a boy that is a friend?

– Exactly!

– And if him, who else? Are there other boys at the pool?

– Of course...

– Or worse. Men. Are there men there at the pool?

– Men?

– Are there predators there at the pool?

– Of course!

– Sick men?

– Brilliant!

– Not like him. Thank you. But really sick men that don't know the difference between a movie on the internet and his daughter there in a bikini. A tight little bikini. Are there men that might see her and think... and feel... you know?

– Yes!

– Not men like him, but sick men.

– Yes! Sick men! Great!

– And suddenly they are everywhere! Everywhere he looks!

– At the pool!

– In the park!

– In the school!

– In the church!

– In the home!

– In the home!

– In the mirror!

– Yes! Yes!

– And suddenly he wants to let the fire burn! He wants to set it off to burn out all the psychos and freaks and degenerates because the world is fucked! Because in that moment he truly believes the world is totally fucked!

– Totally fucked!

– And he can't help but think if he goes to fight that something terrible is going to happen to his little girl!

– Yes! Yes! Something terrible! Yes! And she. Too young to really know it. To understand what that look in his eyes is really all about…

– Yes!

– Feels a deep sense of terrifying dread!

– Brilliant!

– Is that about right?

– Absolutely!

– Thank you!

– So they stand there in the terrible heat with hundreds of people surrounding them waiting for someone to relieve the anger. To put wind back in their sails after a day so long it feels it will never end and as the smoke of the fires circling the city fills the air and all these thoughts and things are swirling

– Raging...

– Yes! Raging through the heat, they...

– They...

– He...

– He thinks about all this and he

– He rushes?

– He rushes at her?

– He rushes?

– And?

– And?

– He thinks about the terrifying state of the decaying world and he screams and rushes at her and...

– And?

– Screams loud and angry and rushes at her and picks her up and

12: SACRIFICE # 1

You want me to

Yes
If you

To tell you

Yes.

Right.

If you don't mind.

No.

Really?

Sure.

Thank you.

But
Why?

Why?

Why would you

Want to?

Yes.
Want to know something like that?

Why would I want to know something like that?

Yes.

It's just
I wonder
Yes?
I just wonder.

Wonder?

Yes.

Right.

Is that okay?

Sure.
I mean
But sure.

Thanks.

Well

Yes?

Well
You take a knife.

Right.

A big one.
Sharp.

Of course.

You come up
You have to come at them from behind.

Right.

With the knife.

Yes.

So they don't
Come up at them in a way where they don't
You know
Have time to react.

Of course.
Quickly.

Right.

Well
I mean kind of quickly
But more

Yes?

More
With purpose
Yes?

Right.

With intent.

Okay.

And you

Yes?

You come up behind them and you

Right
Yes?

And you sit on them.

Sorry?

You sit on their back
Like

Oh.

Like you were going to ride them or
Or something.
Yes?

Really?

Yes.

Okay
Sure

So you sit on them and

Yes

And put your weight on them
So they
So they buckle under you
Yes?

Right.

Collapse

Right.

Collapse under your weight
Yes?

Yes
I

So you come up
Come up from behind and push them
Get them in a position where you can
Where you can sit on them
Push your weight onto them so they buckle
So they buckle under you
And you need to
From that position
You need to lift their head up

Like
Pull it?

Yes
Pull the head towards you.
You grab under
Under the chin

And pull their head up towards you
Hard

Hard?

Yes
You need to
You have to have a good grip
Yes?

Right.

Because they won't just

No
Of course

And so
With the knife

Yes?

You need to slice
To get right into the wind pipe.
So you need to slice pretty deeply

Right

To cut the throat.
Yes?

Right.
Do they
Sorry
Do they fight much?

Well
You know
That's why you sit on them
Yes?

Of course.

But actually
When you cut
It's like they kick and fight more when you're trying to sit on them
Than when you

Really?

Yes.

Right.

So you cut
And you need to
Deep
You need to get pretty deep.

Right.

Right in there
You know?

Okay.

And then the blood
It gushes

Gushes?

Yes.
Really
For at least a minute
Gushes out.
And you need to
You have to hold the head right back
So you can
The whole time
So the blood can come out onto
The ground
Onto the ground.

And they don't struggle?

Not as much as you might
I mean that's if you do it right.

Of course.

They gurgle.

Gurgle?

Make a kind of gurgling noise
Yes.

Right.

But that's just the blood.

Yes.

And then

Yes?

Then they do shake.

Shake?
What do you

After a minute or so they
They kick and shake
Every time.
Once their blood has
But it's just the nerves dying
It's not
It's just the nervous system shutting down
Yes?

Really?

Yes.
It's the death throes.

Right.

So…

Are you
Are you okay?

What?

Are you?

Yes.
Of course.

Are you sure?

Yes.
Why wouldn't

Okay.

I be?

Okay.
That's
Okay.

I

Yes?

I'm not

What?

I don't know if I can do this.

What?

I don't know.

You get it under control is what you

Yes.

Sorry.
You're right.

So you get it under

No. It's just

Just what?

I'm not sure
I feel I don't have any choice but to
Because the thought
The

It means you have to do this.

Yes.

Doesn't it?

Yes.

Because not doing it?

Not doing it means her.
Means…

Yes?

means…

Yes.
So…

No.
It's okay.
I'm okay.
Nothing's wrong.
I'm getting it under

Nothing's wrong?

No.

Don't disappoint me.

Don't worry.

Right.

I'm fine.

Really?

Yes.
Really.
Thanks.

Thanks?

Yes
Thanks.

Right.
So
Then they're
You cut the throat and then they're…

Right.

Thanks.

Right.

Oh

Yes?

Sorry
You must
You have to put your hand in their blood

Sorry?

You have to put your hand in their blood.

Really?

Yes.

Why?

For
And wipe it
Smear it
The blood
On the door to your home.
For protection.

Really?

Yes.
That's how you get protection.

By smearing the blood?

Yes.

Right.
Thank you.

And you're fine?

Yes.

Okay.

Yes.
I'm fine.
Thank you.

CHORUS: *'Behold the Maiden on Her Way'*

It's night. I pull up. Turn the siren off. Leave the lights on. I block a lane. I see it up ahead and I pull up and leave the lights on flashing and try and at least block this one lane. Cars. They are everywhere. Their headlights. Flying. Evacuating. Because of the fires. Horns. Horns trailing off as the cars come up behind me and quickly pull into another lane. Don't they see my lights? My flashing lights? I get out. I step out of the car and into the lane ahead of me. I can feel the cars. On either side. Feel them rushing past. I have left my headlights on and I walk up to it in front of me. The deer. She's young. Not yet adult. She is lying there on the road. A deer? What on earth is a deer doing lying here on the road? She. As I walk up to her she sees me and tries pulling herself away. Using her front hooves to try and pull herself away but it's hopeless. Her back legs are broken. Smashed apart. She... A car flies by with its horn on and I feel it almost hit me. It is so close that it almost runs straight into me. Bastard. Idiot. I call on the radio. It's clipped to my shoulder and I call on the radio to try and get through to dispatch but it's too noisy. I can't hear a thing. The deer. It's still trying to get away from me. Moving towards the next lane. It must. It probably tried to flee the forests. To flee the fires. If I could just get through to dispatch they could send out some more cars. Block the highway off. Send out an animal expert. But with the evacuation... with everyone so desperate... I move up to it. Standing right above it. Its eyes. Its black eyes still showing some tiny flicker of pain and the reflection of the flames in the distance. As if it is trying to tell me. Plead with me to help it. But still scared. Scared of me. Scared of the road. Then. Suddenly. A truck. The huge noise of a truck roars past and I'm knocked off my feet. Knocked backwards off my feet and almost fall into the other lane. I look up from the ground and see cars flying at me. I scramble. Scramble out of their way as wheels rush past my head. This is not good. This is not safe. I can't wait. I must do something. I get back on my feet. I go back up to the deer. She struggles. Her ears back. She desperately struggles to get to her feet and escape but her legs are so... her back legs are just crushed. Completely. I have to do this. I take out my gun. I take out my gun and point it at the deer. I try and wait for a break in the traffic and I take out my gun and point it at the deer's head and pull the trigger and blood. And its blood splatters onto the road. Cars fly past. I try and call in the shots. Scream into the radio 'shots fired'. Procedure. It's procedure. Shots fired. The deer. It starts to shake. It starts to violently shake and roll and thrash about. And as it does that. As it shakes violently. A wind. Suddenly a terrible wind starts blowing from nowhere. Howling. Billowing. Knocking me. Almost making me fall to the ground. A violent and terrible wind.

With the cars and the wind and the deer still shaking on the ground, I try shooting it again. And again. Shots fired. Shots fired. It shakes and thrashes and throws itself round and the wind gets louder and louder and I feel this... this chaos... this sudden sense of chaos and just then another unit pulls up. Another car. Blocking another lane. I shot it, I say. I had to shoot it. I shot it in the head. I say. I scream it. I scream it out. Over the noise of the traffic and the terrible wind. I killed it! I had to kill it! SHOTS FIRED! I HAD TO SHOOT IT! And I look back at her. Barely thirteen I would say. This little girl. On the road. Like she was running across the highway. She has these boots on and a mini-skirt but she could barely be more than thirteen or fourteen years old and if I didn't do that. If I didn't shoot her, the way she was going... The was she was stumbling, who knows what might have happened? If I didn't shoot her who knows how it would have ended? Who knows?

13: SACRIFICE # 2

– The flames.

– The heat.

– Rushing. It's rushing.

– The flames and the heat are rushing all around him.

– The sound.

– The fierce and terrifying sound.

– The town…

– Suddenly the town is burning.

– Just like that.

– The wall of flames roars down the hill and now the entire town is
  burning.

– Chaos.

– Chaos burns all around him.

– Smoke.

– Flames.

– Fire.

– Chaos.

– Billowing chaos everywhere he looks.

– He sees her screaming.

– He sees her crying.

– Through the deafening sounds of the fire he sees her trying to cry
  out to him from the car he bought her so she could learn to drive.

– The car on fire.

– Bursting with flames.

– Paint blistering.

– Tyres melting.

– What does he do?

– What can he do?

– He has to save her.

– He has to do something.

– But his radio blares at him.

– He sees his daughter's silent screams of deep fear from the burning car as his radio blares at him.

– The radio is not about his daughter.

– The radio is about the town. Hundreds of people. Hundreds of people screaming for his help. Desperate for the help only he can provide.

– The entire town.

– Him the captain of the local fire squad.

– His daughter.

– The town.

– The fire.

– The heat.

– The car.

– His love.

– Their love.

– Hundreds of people huddled on the town oval as the fire surrounds them.

– What does he do? What can he do?

– He sees her through the window.

– He sees her through the window of the car.

– The car she had run to, to try to escape.

– To try to escape the flames and the fire.

– That now traps her.

– That is now damning her.

– He sees the flames peeling the paint.

– He sees her beating against the glass of the window, screaming for him.

– His radio blares at him. Pleading with him to get to the oval as soon as he can.

– No.

– He can't.

– He can't go.

– He has to save her.

– He desperately tries to find a way to get to her. He goes to the car. The flames surrounding it are so hot he can't get close to it. He tries to push through the pain. His daughter. This is for his daughter. But each time his body pulls him back. He is crying and screaming and he tries to do something... anything... but all he can do is stand there and watch her scream for his help as his radio wails about the hundreds of people in great danger that need him to do his job... That need him to know what the right thing to do is...

– He steps back from the car.

– He backs away from her.

– He can't save her.

– He stumbles back.

– All his years of training.

– All the people and homes he has saved.

– Everything he has endured.

– Everything for nothing.

– He looks at her.

– She is like an animal. A wild animal. The fear. The desperation.

– She sees her father step back.

– She sees her father give up.

– They look into each other's eyes.

– They look deep into each other's eyes.

– He mouths he loves her.

– She stops screaming.

– She stops beating.

– She doesn't feel the flames.

– He watches them swallow her.

– He sees her disappear into them

– He sees her die.

– He turns.

– He walks away.

– He runs.

– He turns his back and runs down the main street to the oval and feels

– Where hundreds are relying on him.

– Where no-one knows what he has just had to do.

– Where he needs to be a hero.

– As he runs he hears the car explode and at that moment he is filled with…

– He never heard her screams.

– She saw him give up.

– As he runs the chaos that surrounds him enters into him.

– He couldn't hear her cries.

– As he runs from his dead daughter and hears the explosion from the car and knows she is now nothing but fire, the chaos that has been billowing around him, enters him. Enters his lungs. Enters his skin. Makes its way deep into his blood until there is nothing of him left. Nothing of the hero. Of the father. Of the husband. There is nothing but the chaos. He is nothing but chaos. Everything is chaos.

14: SACRIFICE # 3

We see a fawn being killed by hand, much like in the description in 'Sacrifice # 1'.

Epilogue: Iphigenia replies…

– Kiss me mother kiss your darlin'
Lay my head upon your breast
Throw your loving arms around me
I am weary let me rest

Seems the light is swiftly fading
Brighter scenes they do now show
I am standing by the river
Angels wait to take me home

Kiss me mother kiss your darlin'
See the pain upon my brow
While I'll soon be with the angels
Fate has doomed my future now

Through the years you've always loved me
And my life you've tried to save
But now I shall slumber sweetly
In a deep and lonely grave

Kiss me mother kiss your darlin'
Lay my head upon your breast
Throw your loving arms around me
I am weary let me rest
I am weary let me rest! *

END OF PLAY

---

* 'I Am Weary (Let Me Rest)', traditional American folk song performed by the Cox Family in the Cohen Brothers film 'O Brother, Where Art Thou?' (2000).